The

AN EARLY BIRD BOOK™

Written by Margaret Lane
Illustrated by David Nockels

Random House New York

The roar of a lion in the African night is one of the most thrilling sounds in the world. It is also frightening. The lion is proclaiming that the territory he is in – forest, jungle, or plain – is his alone, and that intruders will be killed.

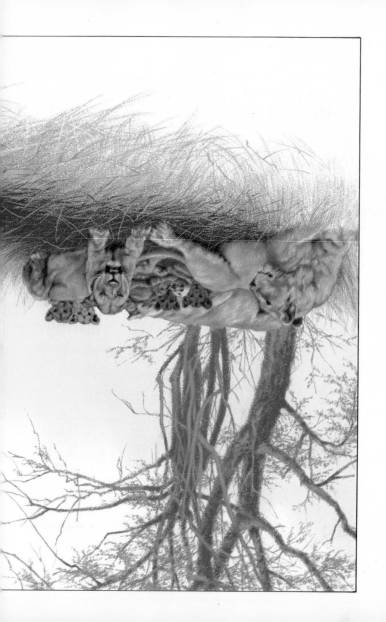

The lion lives with his family, which is called a pride. There may be one or two other related males, but most of the company will be females and their cubs. The lionesses, too, are all related – sisters, cousins, aunts.

Lions live entirely upon meat, and need plenty. Prey must be pursued and killed, which is not easy. Lions usually have a dinner about twice a week, if they are lucky, and a surprise attack at a water hole is their best chance of catching a drinking wildebeest or giraffe.

The females are the real hunters of the family. For most of the day they lie hidden in the shade, or resting on the branch of a tree, where there are fewer flies. They may seem to be fast asleep, but if a herd of zebra or wildebeest comes in sight, and they are hungry, they prepare stealthily to attack.

This requires skill and speed, for grazing animals are alert and gallop fast. More often than not they escape. Lionesses work together in twos or threes, circling and stalking their prey. Then one, lying hidden in the grass, dashes in for the kill.

This is the moment when the lion,
king of the pride, moves in for his share.
The lionesses and cubs must wait while
he has his fill, or he will snarl and
threaten. Then the females and cubs can
eat what is left, before hyenas, jackals,
and vultures sneak in to pick the bones.

After a good meal – fifty pounds or more of meat in their full stomachs – the lions must drink. This they do at a stream or water hole, lapping up water with their tongues, like ordinary house cats. It may take twenty minutes of drinking to satisfy their thirst. When that is done they can lie in the long grass and sleep for hours.

The two or three male lions in a pride are usually brothers. They patrol the territory, which they often do at night, sleeping lazily during the day. The lion's bulky mane makes him look even larger than he is, and helps to protect him in a fight with a rival lion or other enemy.

When a lioness has mated and is pregnant, she retires to a hidden place where the cubs are born. There are usually three or four in a litter, soft and fluffy, with speckled fur and amber-colored eyes. Their mother nurses them, and soon they are as playful and mischievous as kittens.

Every few days the lioness moves
her cubs, to hide them from jackals and
hyenas. After a few weeks she carries
them back to the pride, holding them
carefully by the scruff of the neck.
Perhaps only half her little ones will have
survived, for food is scarce and there are
always hungry animals around.

While the lioness is out hunting, the cubs are cared for by her sisters and cousins, the "aunts" of the pride. The lion is too lazy to trouble himself with this, but allows the cubs to romp beside him, even playing with his tail. If they become too bold, however, he will snarl and roar.

Lions keep themselves very clean, licking their fur with their rough tongues. The lioness grooms her cubs until they can do this themselves, and are learning to hunt on their own. The young females will stay with the pride, but the males wander off together for a few years of bachelor life.

In the past, lion and human, hunter and killer, have been enemies. But now the lions that are left live mostly in nature reserves. They have become used to harmless tourists in cars and usually ignore them. The king of beasts, fierce and proud, must always regard the territory as his own.